G000162619

This advice for washing, cleaning and removing stains
was first published in 1893. This new edition
includes illustrations from a time when
everyday items such as potatoes, old beer, and
walnut juice were considered as indispensable
as the mangles mops and feather brushes.

MANGLES
MOPS
&
FEATHER
BRUSHES

Advice for the Laundry and Spring Cleaning
By
An Experienced Housewife

Copper Beech Publishing

Published in Great Britain by
Copper Beech Publishing Ltd
© Copper Beech Publishing Ltd 1993
New edition published 1999

ISBN 0 9516295 7 3

A CIP catalogue record for this book is available from
The British Library

Copper Beech Publishing Ltd
P O Box 159, East Grinstead,
Sussex RH19 4FS England

CONTENTS

CONTENTS

THE HOUSE CLEANING
Only by strictly adhering to a system can a house be kept in order ...

The housewife will find the only really good plan is to have a thorough cleaning done each day in one or two rooms of the house, so that in a week, or at all events in a fortnight, every nook and corner has been visited by the broom, the feather-brush, the duster and the carpet brush.

One day's work should be the bedrooms, another the dressing-rooms; the next day is given to the dining-room, the next to the drawing-room. The hall, the staircase, the cellars, the attics, must all be kept equally clean, and a day must be appointed for attending to each of them.

It is a universal custom to devote Saturday to the cleaning of the kitchen.

Only by strictly adhering to this system can a house be kept in order.

Dust and dirt have to be fought with all over the premises every day, more quickly perhaps, but in such a manner as to give the whole house an orderly and clean appearance.

Nothing is more ugly than a thin layer of dust ...

Nothing is more uninviting than dust on the wainscot and panels of a room, or a stain of old mud on the floor; to see the tables covered with articles which should be in the cupboards - and cloaks lying on the chairs, instead of being replaced in the wardrobes after they have been worn.

In a large establishment every servant has a special part of the house under her charge to clean weekly, keep in order, and dust lightly every day.

In a small house where only two or three women servants are kept, the cook takes entire charge of the kitchen, the cellars, the hall, and the dining-room if there is no parlour maid.

It is well to map out a week's or a fortnight's cleaning, and write it down upon a paper pinned up in some convenient place. Never allow your servants to deviate from this map, and your house will always be clean and in order.

In cleaning, method and regularity reduce labour very greatly, as no part of the house is allowed ever to get very dirty.

∽⊙⊚∾

When cleaning a room, wash all the mirrors, windows, and any china or crystals in it. Brush the hangings, the papers, the ceilings and cornices.

Pieces of furniture or panellings of wood must be well rubbed after dusting, to obtain a good polish.

If the door of a room is sufficiently large, put all the chairs and couches into the hall or passage - which is always cleaned after the rooms opening on to it.

If one has not the time to dust all the ornaments one possesses, it is far better to put them away in cupboards

Brush all the stuff with which the chairs are covered before bringing them back into the room after the walls and floor are finished. For velvet you require rather a hard brush, and you must be careful to brush it the right way.

Dust with a brush also, all the objects and ornaments of gilded bronze, of copper or brass. Afterwards polish them with a chamois leather. The knobs and handles of the doors should be rubbed and polished.

Vases, whether transparent or opaque, must be carefully washed and make it a daily care to change the water in all vases which hold flowers.

... change the water in all vases which hold flowers, as otherwise it becomes very disagreeable.

⚬⚬⚬

Carpets that are laid so as to cover the whole floor, and nailed down, should always have a layer underneath of strong brown paper, which not only saves the carpet from being worn by the boards, but rejects the dust.

At the half-yearly cleanings ...

At the half-yearly cleanings, when the carpets are taken up, this paper should be swept over with a soft broom before it is moved. The floor underneath will be found perfectly clean, and the paper will be found to have only a little light dust on it if the carpet has been properly cleaned every week. It should be well brushed with a good, long-handled carpet broom - and do not forget in all this work that new brooms not only sweep clean, but do not wear the carpet out so much as old ones!

There is considerable skill needed to brush a carpet well. Many servants brush too heavily and destroy the carpet. This is not necessary if the carpet is well sprinkled before brushing with damp tea-leaves, or better still, as is done on the Continent, with the outside leaves of lettuces and endive, freshly-cut grass or cabbage, or any green stuff.

Where a room or passage is much used, and the carpet is fixed down, it should be washed with Sunlight or Hudson's Soap about four times a year.

There is considerable skill needed to brush a carpet well.
Many servants brush too heavily and destroy the carpet.
This is not necessary if the carpet is well sprinkled before
brushing with damp tea leaves.

*For the walls it is a good plan to use a workman's brush
and a pail of good soapy lather.*

Move the large pieces of furniture, and remove
the dust which has collected behind them. Take
down all the pictures and thoroughly wipe both sides.

Valuable oil paintings require careful cleaning and
a servant should not be allowed to touch them.

Take the opportunity of these half-yearly
derangements of the house to have a coat of white-
wash given to bathrooms, lavatories, sculleries, and
always in the kitchen. This is very inexpensive, and,
will prevent many illnesses in the house. Many
illnesses are carried and caused by the accumulations
of dirt, even of light dust, which are overlooked by
careless housekeepers!

The table used for regular cooking must be
scrubbed every day, after dinner is over.

*Every particle of dust is a particle of danger.
Never forget this, and you will save yourself
much trouble and grief.*

To clean really well it is absolutely necessary to have good tools, and enough of them. You must have:

Brushes of hair,
Dusters,
Feather-brushes large and small
(one with a long handle to touch everything),
Two hard carpet brooms,
One soft short-handled brush for the dust pan,
One soft long-handled one to sweep floors,
Sponges of different sizes,
Cloths to dry and rub with,
A mop, and a good chamois leather,
Plenty of soap, soda, and Sanitas,
A stool and good double steps,
A tin pail and a wooden pail,
A bowl for the lather for the paint,
Two strong scrubbing brushes.

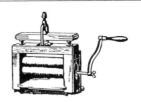

THE HOUSEHOLD LINEN
If you put it in soak every week you can have a regular washing day once a month ...

To wash the linen at home costs less than half what it costs to send it out, and it is much better done.

If you buy the soap in advance, and keep it in a dry place, much less is used than if it is fetched all soft from the grocer at the moment when it is wanted.

❧

I will explain also the advantage of frequent washes. It used to be considered a matter of pride to possess an excessive quantity of linen, and to wash only occasionally. But you miss nothing when you cannot do this.

In making linen it is well to provide more than is necessary - in case of illness, when the usual supply is insufficient.

Do not forget that linen, like everything else, is subject to changes of fashion. Moreover, linen which is kept a long time folded in cupboards without being taken into use, becomes yellow, and cut in the folds; it is wasted like capital that lies idle!

To wash at home you must have certain arrangements made. A wash-house, even if it be very small, is an indispensable necessity, or else everything has to be done in the kitchen, and you cannot hope to wash much at a time.

To steep the linen it is necessary to have a washing tub of galvanised iron, which is placed on a stool close to the copper. Then you have tubs for soaking and for making the lather, trestles or 'horses' on which to place the linen, a shelf on which to keep the soda, the blue, &c. In a handy corner have the coal and wood placed ready to light the fire under your copper.

THE CARE OF THE LINEN
There is no worse plan than to throw the linen in a heap in a corner.

Take care to spread the soiled linen in a garret reserved for it. There is no worse plan than to throw the linen in a heap in a corner.

Hang all the chemises on a cord, or a bar of wood, by themselves, the handkerchiefs on another, &c. Each kind of linen should be separated from the rest, and placed by itself. In this way you prevent from the first the coarse linen being mixed with the fine, the linen which is very dirty with that which is scarcely soiled, as, for instance, sheets and dusters.

There is still another reason for spreading the soiled linen, and which makes it advisable not to leave it long before soaking it, and that is that it quickly takes mould marks if you are not very careful.

If you have not a garret in which to spread it, before throwing into the basket look it over and assure yourself that it is not damp. If it should be, have it well dried before it is put away.

Choose for the soaking one day in the week, and try to keep it always for that purpose. The linen should be two hours at least in the water.

The work is much lightened by this; the linen is cleaned more easily, it needs less rubbing, and is consequently less worn.

When the soaking is finished, examine the linen well to see that it has no spots which have but partly disappeared - spots of rust, spots of damp, spots of mildew, spots of fruit.

After soaking, the trouble and fatigue of the washing are much lessened.

*When the soaking is finished, examine the linen well
to see that it has no spots which have
but partly disappeared...*

HOW TO REMOVE SPOTS FROM LINEN

Spots of Damp

Dip the spot in butter-milk or put on the spot a little lemon juice or salt. Place it immediately afterwards in the hot sun. If you see that the stain shows while it is still wet, soap it immediately or cover the stain with chalk finely powdered, and rub well.

Spots of Rust

Moisten the spot, cover it with powdered salt of sorrel, and put it in the sun. Rinse it several times, as the oxalic acid is poison. Or place the spot in the steam of boiling water, then cover with salt and lemon juice.

Stains of fruit or tea

Spots produced by fruit or by tea can be taken out by boiling water, which you sprinkle over it while another person holds the stuff out tight.

Stains of Ink

If you happen to stain your linen with ink in the grape season, rub the spots with the juice of sour grapes. If you cannot have grape juice, some leaves of sorrel should be pounded on the spots.

If you are without that useful garden herb, the juice of ripe tomatoes will make a good substitute.

Afterwards use the powdered salt of sorrel. Rub gently over the surface you have made wet. Plunge the linen afterwards in fresh water and rinse well.

Old Stains

If the stains are very old, wrap up in the spot a piece of salt of sorrel, not powdered. Soak in lukewarm water and leave until the salt has melted. The stain will then have disappeared. I repeat the caution given before - be sure you rinse the linen well in fresh water.

Acids

Stains due to acids should be treated by alkalines.

Spots of Grease

There are often spots of grease which will resist any washing. These must be dipped in treacle, and afterwards well rinsed.

Linen which has become Yellow

Linen which has become yellow in the cupboards can be bleached in the following manner:

Take a pound of white soap and cut up on the fire in four pints of milk. When the soap is melted put the linen in the copper, and let it boil for half-an-hour. Take it out and wash it in soapy water. Rinse in two waters, with blue in the last.

Linen which has become singed

To restore linen which has been singed, cut a large onion in slices and extract the juice by pressing or pounding it. Add to the juice one ounce of soap, a pint of vinegar, and one ounce of Fuller's earth. The compound is put on the fire till it is just boiling. Then spread the mixture on the spots, leave it to dry and complete the cleaning with soapy water.

THE WASH

**Let us suppose you are ready for
your washing day ...**

*L*inen well soaked and arranged in order is ready to wash whenever you choose. One last caution - every piece ought to be marked; this will save a world of trouble and the loss of many articles.

Before putting linen in the wash check it by a list. Write the number of articles in a little book and when the linen is brought back, assure yourself that the same articles are brought back as were taken.

❧

The night before the wash, place the tub on the tripod or stool. The soaked linen is wet in a bucket, and arranged in heaps, by the lists, in the washing tub. At the bottom should be a layer of dusters - soaked like the rest, spread on long pieces of orris-root.

The linen ought not to touch the bottom of the tub and between the heaps of linen you place the strands of orris-root. Finish by a thick heap of dusters, and cover the whole with a very coarse cloth.

You prepare the wash in this way on the evening before the scalding: use rain-water if possible, which adds greatly to the cleansing power. Put the crystals of soda to melt and the sifted charcoal into a closed linen bag. Let the solution boil well in the brick-work copper which is built over the fire.

∽◉◊◉◟

The next morning, light the fire early and make the water hot. You should work with a copper spoon which has a very long handle.

Pour the water in around the washing-tub. After having run through the linen, the water falls into a bucket, from which you throw it again into the copper. Increase the heat of the water every time you let it pass through, pouring it on boiling last.

The scalding continues according to the quantity of the linen.

When all is finished, cover the washing tub again with a kind of carpet in thick wool, and shut the mouth at the bottom. The linen is thus kept in a warm moisture which greatly assists in cleaning it.

The next day put the linen into baskets to be washed in fresh water.

Rinse well, and then put everything in blue except the dusters.

If you use the ball blue, tie up a piece of it in the leg of an old white cotton stocking. If you prefer the liquid blue, here is a receipt for its preparation:

A Good Receipt for Liquid Blue.

To one pint of clear rain water, one ounce of powdered Prussian blue and a very little oxalic acid. A teaspoonful of the mixture is enough for a large bucket of water.

I know a laundress who never uses chloride or soap.
She replaces these materials by boiled potatoes,
with which she rubs the linen.

Whenever it is possible, it is out of doors
that you must spread all the linen
that comes in contact with the body.

DRYING
To dry the linen, nothing is so good as the open air.

*W*henever it is possible, it is out of doors that you must spread all the linen that comes in contact with the body. The sun and the wind clean and destroy impurities which linger in linen that has been worn. People who have a tendency to diseases of the skin should *never* neglect this precaution.

⌘

When the weather makes it impossible to spread the linen out of doors, the only plan is to dry it in a garret. Take care that the garret is well cleaned and that all the dust has been taken up with a wet duster.

It is taken for granted that you have your attics in good order and properly arranged.

THE WASHING OF PRINTED CLOTHS AND MUSLINS

Black stockings should be plunged into water to which has been added a little walnut juice ...

On days other than the special washing day, you can do washings of a less serious character.

Petticoats, collars, shirt fronts, wristbands, which can be washed successfully with other things, must be left to get whiter, if their colour is not good.

The American manner of soaping them is very good. Take fifty pints of water too hot to touch and four pounds of soap. Add six middle-sized spoonsful of alkali, and two of essence of turpentine. Mix all with the aid of a little brush. Plunge the linen in and leave it for five hours. Cover the tub closely.

I have given the quantities for a great deal of linen; for a small amount reduce the proportions.

Afterwards wash the linen, rubbing it gently: take it out of the first water, and pour boiling water over it, then rinse it. The linen will be beautifully white, and it is much less worn as it needs very little rubbing.

The ammonia evaporates immediately: the smell of the turpentine disappears entirely in drying. It is that essence which gives the whiteness to the linen.

❧

Fine muslins should be steeped for half-an-hour in warm water in which a tablespoonful of borax to four quarts of water has been dissolved.

Rub afterwards in a lather obtained by pouring boiling water on white soft soap; the lather should be allowed to get cold after it has thickened. Muslins are rinsed by pressing them with the hands. They must not be wrung out.

Art-muslins and laces and embroidered tulles should first be well shaken to get rid of the dust with which they will probably be covered.

Black stockings which are very dirty should be plunged into water to which has been added a little walnut juice, and washed afterwards. Then rinse in hard water slightly vinegared.

All delicate fancy stockings, when new, should be put into salted water and left to steep for some hours. They should never be worn until they have been submitted to this process.

WASHING FLANNELS AND WOOLLENS
**The water of haricot beans is valuable on
account of the starch which it contains ...**

To wash your flannels, dissolve one ounce of
carbonate of soda in a tub of water. Steep the articles
for twelve hours. Stretch the flannel every way and
wash in another tub of water where you have melted
a large spoonful of wheat flour. The flannel will come
out clean and soft, not shrunk or thickened.

The water of haricot beans, which some persons
use for washing flannels, is valuable for this purpose
on account of the starch which it contains.

❧❧❧

Berlin wool work gets dirty very quickly. You
can clean it by plunging it into a lather of soap, and
stirring it well.

You should hang up the things to drip, stretching them out and rolling them lengthways to keep their shape. They must be stretched out to dry.

Indian wool: it is necessary to take the wool while in the hank and wash it in boiling water, before you begin to work with it.

⁕

We cannot leave the laundry without setting it in order. Rinse out and wipe the washing tub so that it does not rust. When it is quite dry cover it. The water from the washing is very good to use for cleaning floors and stones. It will keep well for a day or two.

Sweep the floor, arrange the trestles or horses against the wall, and hang up the baskets. Place on the shelf the stone jars containing black soap and soda, the bottles of Javel water (bleaching liquid), and the blue in balls or in liquid. Hang up the branches of orris. The buckets must be so arranged that their bottoms do not touch the wall or the floor.

When you have finished the laundry should be in as good order as any other part of the house.

INSPECTION OF LINEN, AND
PREPARING IT FOR IRONING
Fold carefully – and with taste

When the linen has been brought back to the linen room, it must be looked over before it is ironed. When you do not wash at home you must leave that inspection until the laundress returns.

The examination should be thorough. Articles which require darning, mending, or repairing in any way, are folded and put into a separate basket. Those which need nothing are put ready for ironing.

Chemises, vests, drawers, &c, fold inside out. Shake and stretch them ready for smoothing; then fold them at once, and place in a different basket from those which have to be mended.

It is well to separate the linen according to the lists, at the time when they are being got ready; putting together all the chemises, in another heap placing the shirts, in another the petticoats, &c.

In ironing, keep sets of things together. Stretch the dusters and cloths both ways, fold all long ways, with the mark or stripe to show outside.

Chamber towels ought to be perfectly dry before they are put away. Stretch them also; it is better than ironing. Fold carefully, and with taste, so as to show the embroidered marks, or the edges of lace.

Stretch all cloths and table-cloths; the last must be stretched by two persons, then carefully placed, folded, in the basket of things ready for ironing.

Sheets also must be stretched by two persons. It is best to place them in pairs. When the two sheets have been folded separately, put the hems together and place them one inside the other, so that the two form but one.

All sheets trimmed with lace or embroidery *must* be ironed.

Stretch all the ordinary socks and stockings. Roll them together in pairs. For these, also, numbering is essential to avoid confusion! Fold them inside out, so as to enable the foot to go properly in when they are put on, then roll them, bringing outside that part of the leg which has the mark. Fine socks and stockings must be ironed, inside out.

Before ironing the linen, damp it slightly. Do not moisten more than you are sure you will iron during the day. Have the water in a jar or bowl, and sprinkle every article with the hand, then roll it up and put it again in the basket for ironing. This should be done an hour before the ironing begins. This is necessary in order to give a good polish to the linen.

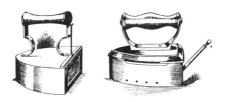

*For your gentlemen's shirts, you must
employ hot starch. The hotter it is,
the better the linen will look ...*

STARCHING

... that most difficult and delicate of tasks, ironing gentlemen's shirts ...

Starching must be done very carefully. There are several methods of giving a good gloss. One laundress that I know adds always half an ounce of stearine to a pint of prepared starch. She lets the mixture boil for three minutes. It makes a magnificent starch.

Another receipt is to pour a quarter of a pint of boiling water on one ounce of gum arabic, then cover the basin and leave it for the night. A teaspoonful of the preparation is put into every pint of starch.

◦⟨⊙⟩◦

An ironer of great experience teaches this mode of obtaining a perfect success, which would satisfy the most fastidious. It is for that most difficult and delicate of tasks, ironing gentlemen's shirts.

Dissolve in a teacup of water - sufficiently warm to melt the starch, but not hot enough to curdle it - a good ounce of pure wax and double the quantity of borax; add three teacups of pulverised starch, and pass through a sieve. To use it take a teaspoonful, which you dissolve in water.

But first, for your gentlemen's shirts, you must employ hot starch. That starch must never be too thick: the hotter it is, the better the linen will look. The more it is rubbed, the better also.

When it will absorb no more, apply the starch on the wrong side. If the starch does not spread well, the iron sticks, and leaves the linen swollen and spotty.

After having used the hot starch, plunge the article in cold water, to which you have added a teaspoonful of the composition described above. Wring, and rub gently. An hour after, rub very carefully with a linen cloth wrung out in hot water, to equalise the surface, then spread over the starched linen a thin cloth, through which you give the first pressure of the iron. When you draw away the cloth damp the starched linen again a very little, and finally iron with care.

The ironer folds the linen all alike;
all the pieces should have the same shape, both in
length and width, and the same folds ...

IRONING

The irons used should be sufficiently thick not to get cold very quickly.

The ironing table must be of a certain width, and it should be high enough to prevent the ironer from stooping, as to bend over an ironing table produces needless backache and headache.

A board which stands on the trestles, is very valuable if you have not a regular linen room, because it can be put longways against the wall on its supports, and takes very little room.

Moreover, the board is convenient, indeed it is indispensable, for ironing dress-skirts and petticoats. You place it inside the skirt, and only in this way can you iron such an article of dress without making ugly folds.

Another small board is very useful for the little daily ironings, for pressing seams, &c. The little board should be hung on two hooks, by two rings of leather nailed on the back.

The ironer folds the linen all alike; all the pieces of the same dozen should have the same shape, both in length and width, and the same folds.

The irons used should be sufficiently thick not to get cold very quickly. Keep them polished and bright. You can have them bright and clear as glass by rubbing them, when they are hot, with a little bit of bees' wax enclosed in a linen bag, then drying with a cloth sprinkled with salt.

Every time you take an iron from the fire, dry with a cloth. When you want to put it down, place it on a support - a little grille on four feet - so as not to burn the table cover or the board.

The person who mends the linen, smooths it, folds it, irons it, or later on, puts it away, must have very clean hands. A clean apron must cover the dress.

THE PUTTING AWAY OF THE LINEN
... a little elegance which is very cheap and very charming.

*Y*ou have only now to put the linen away! For keeping it you have one or more cupboards in the linen room or elsewhere.

Linen cupboards must be made to shut tight; and before putting the linen away, be sure to dust the shelves with a clean towel.

I have seen linen cupboards of which the shelves were edged with a border of embroidery pasted to the wood. The table napkins and towels of different sets were tied together in their right order, with broad, rose-coloured satin ribbon - a little elegance which is very cheap and very charming.

The linen cupboard properly so-called contains the sheets, the pillow cases, and the chamber towels.

Personal linen is put away in the bedrooms or dressing-rooms; the kitchen towels, dusters, hand-towels and cooking aprons in the kitchen or house-keeper's room.

Put away the linen in good order, ready to put your hand on it at any moment without confusion.

The pairs of sheets are piled in order, one under the other. Arrange them so that one does not reach out further than another. The table linen should be placed on different shelves from the towels and pillow cases, or in another cupboard. Chamber towels must *not* be mixed with them.

The same rules of taste and order should observed for personal linen. Put together the fine chemises in ribbons, by the dozen; handkerchiefs and drawers the same.

The kitchen linen should be arranged with the same care, if not so elaborately.

Lavender gives a delicious odour to the linen. Dry it in the shade, and then put it into bags of muslin and put it about in the cupboards and drawers.

THE CARE OF THE LINEN
Very few persons know how to sew on a button

A wise housewife who understands true economy inspects the linen cupboard at least once a year. She makes notes of what changes must be effected, and additions made, to keep the linen in good order.

It is much better to replace as quickly as possible the things that are worn out, so that the others, which are in good condition are not over-worked.

What a care the linen is to a housewife worthy of the name! Little things in the household take up so much of our time, cost so dear, demand so much attention.

Thus the mendings must be careful, and the smallest attended to at once. Buttons must be replaced and hems or seams must be resewn straight away.

> **How to sew on a button
> to hold for a long time.**

Very few persons know how to sew on a button so that it will hold a long time and not drag away the piece of stuff on which it is sewn.

Before putting the button on the stuff, sew it across with thread, in such a way that the knot at the end of the needleful remains on the right side of the stuff, and consequently under the button. This alone will hinder the button being carried away by the iron.

When you begin to sew on the button, place under it, crossways, a pin, round which you pass the thread every time, drawing it out when you have finished. It is necessary to turn the thread several times under the button, so as to form a cord that will sustain the wear and tear of use.

It is very unusual for buttons put on like this to come off.

These are some of the little things, but they have their importance. Who has not witnessed the annoyance and impatience of the male members of a family when a button gives way? Why not try to save these trials for them, and for oneself?

⸻

Sheets which are beginning to wear in the middle should be turned. Join the two selvages at the edge, so as to form a centre less worn. If the sheet is whip-stitched, that stitching will have to be picked out first, and the simple selvages united. If the sheet is without seam, make one in the middle the full length.

When too old for use, sheets should be cut up into dusters. But often, before they descend so low, they can be converted into sheets for children's beds.

If you have more linen than you need, then give some away to your poor friends, who are always thankful for such necessary things.

Linen is expensive, but it renders great services while still a thread of it exists.

USEFUL RECEIPTS

THE CARE OF THE FURNITURE

To take out the stains of candle grease without damaging polished wood, use a little hot water and a rag.

Polished tables are sometimes stained by syrups, liqueurs, lemonades: if water is not enough to take away these spots, clean with a lukewarm decoction of coffee-dregs. Rub well, dry with some soft linen and afterwards use a polish.

White stains upon polished furniture are taken away by holding a hot plate over the stains.

When furniture has been bruised, soak the damaged part with warm water. Apply a piece of brown paper, five or six times doubled, and also saturated with warm water. Pass over the paper a hot iron, until nearly all the moisture has evaporated. If the bruise is a deep one, it is necessary to soak with warm water, and to put close to the surface a hot iron, keeping the bruise damp during some minutes, and without taking away the iron.

USEFUL RECEIPTS

THE CARE OF THE FLOORS

*B*efore spreading any wax or paste on a polished floor, wash it thoroughly, and let it get quite dry. Then spread over it the following mixture, prepared the night before. Cut up the bees' wax into wafers, and throw the bits into a pot. Cover entirely with essence of turpentine. Leave it all night in that state. Tomorrow the mixture will form a thick paste. Take a morsel of cloth, and rub the floor all over with it. When the paste is dry, rub the boards with a brush.

To preserve the polish of the floor, rub it every morning with a piece of woollen cloth, which is soaked twice a week in petroleum oil. Brush the floor backwards and forwards.

When the floor is stained with grease, put on some strong essence of turpentine, and then some powdered talc. Keep on the talc for a few moments and iron, just hot enough. Put afterwards the polishing paste on the spot that has been cleaned.

USEFUL RECEIPTS

LEATHER AND CANE CHAIRS

To refresh the leather of chairs and other articles of furniture, rub it with the white of an egg, well beaten.

Clean cane chairs in this way; first, take off the dust, then wash the seats all over, but *underneath* only with warm water. Dry them in the open air. You should choose a sunny day. Best chairs will come up like new and last so a long time.

CARPETS AND HANGINGS

It is undeniable that carpets give to a house a comfortable and elegant appearance; it is equally undeniable that they furnish it as nothing else does; but they are a great expense, and to look well take a great deal of care.

To clean the carpets well, many people employ, from time to time, certain substances which take out the spots and revive the colours.

USEFUL RECEIPTS

Some sprinkle with wheat flour and salt, which they brush away afterwards, with the rest of the dirt.

Others brush the carpet then wipe with a clean cloth soaked in salt water.

Tea leaves are found very good for this purpose, but they should not be used if the colours of the carpet are very light or clear.

Damp bran is preferable. Pour cold water on the bran, and let it steep for half an hour. Press it well with the hands, until it is nearly dry, then pour it on the carpet and brush afterwards. Or you can use damp grass; all spots and dust will be removed and the colours will revive brilliantly.

Ammonia also restores the colours of a carpet. You throw an ordinary spoonful into four quarts of water.

If soot is spilled on the carpet, sprinkle over it salt, and brush. No trace of the soot will be left.

USEFUL RECEIPTS

When it is necessary to wash a loose carpet, shake it first, then beat it well. Afterwards stretch it out firmly. Then prepare a mixture composed of calf's gall and three and a half or four pints of cold soft water, or water that has been softened. Steep a flannel in the mixture, and rub the carpet well with it. Wash the floor before putting down the carpet, and leave it to dry. Then put the carpet down, but *do not allow anyone to walk over it till it is perfectly dry.*

When you leave the house for a long absence, the carpets are in great danger from moths and grubs. To protect them prepare the following mixture. Take three pints of clean water, and three spoonfuls of essence of turpentine. Brush the carpet well then saturate a sponge with the mixture, pressing it so that it should not be too wet. Pass it over every part of the carpet. When the water becomes dirty, prepare a fresh mixture. It is surprising how that operation cleans the carpets and disinfects them.

USEFUL RECEIPTS

FLOOR-COVERINGS OF LINOLEUM

For the cleaning of these floor-coverings use a piece of woollen stuff, or a piece of knitting. They last much longer if cleaned in that way, and keep their appearance a long while. To get into good order a floor cloth which has been frequently washed, heat some sweet oil, and rub well the surface to bring back its flexibility.

WINDOWS AND MIRRORS

When window-panes or mirrors have been streaked by some accident, you can take out the marks by applying saffron powder which has been diluted in a few drops of spirits of wine. Rub afterwards with a chamois leather.

USEFUL RECEIPTS

To clean window-panes or mirrors, the following methods are equally good. Reduce to powder a little bit of indigo; take up the powder with a soft damp cloth. Rub on the window-panes and wash afterwards. Some persons clean the mirrors with petroleum. Then moths do not approach them. A sponge can be used. Polish afterwards with old newspapers.

If a mirror has been splashed with oil or grease, the spots disappear if you rub them with a slice of onion.

N.B. - Be careful that for plate glass or mirrors you never use ribbed cloths.

PAPER HANGINGS

$\mathcal{P}$aper hangings are cleaned with a flannel tied round a long-handled brush.

Grease marks on paper hangings throw careful and order-loving housewives into despair! Take them out by applying a paste of cold water and Fuller's earth. Leave it all night. If the spots remain, they are too old; a second application will make all right.

USEFUL RECEIPTS

CLEANING GILT FRAMES

To preserve gilt frames from being spotted by flies, coat them over with oil of laurel.

Gilt frames are cleaned well, and rendered very brilliant, by the following procedure:

Wash very gently and carefully, with a little sponge soaked in spirits of wine and essence of turpentine. The sponge should be only damp. Do not dry afterwards.

You can rub gently to take off the spots with a bit of flannel damped with white of egg.

Or, apply old beer to the frames with a soft rag.

To keep flies out of rooms, in which they always leave disagreeable traces of their presence, place in every room the following mixture: half a teaspoonful of white pepper, one of brown sugar, one of cream, well mixed - or strong green tea well sweetened; or a teaspoonful of laudanum on shavings of quassia thrown into boiling water. The flies will disappear.

USEFUL RECEIPTS

CLEANING GILDED BRONZES

*W*ash the bronze with a brush dripping with water; afterwards pass over the object a brush dipped in the following mixture: water, two ounces; nitric acid, half an ounce; a very small pinch of alum. Dry in the sun, or by a moderate fire.

Here is a mixture for taking fly spots from bronzes: oil of lavender, an eighth of an ounce; alcohol, three quarters of an ounce; water, half an ounce. Use a soft sponge and rub well; work rapidly.

A weak soapy water, or an ammoniated water, cleans statues and ornaments of bronze, in the fine lines, where dust accumulates, and which must be kept as clean as possible by frequent brushings.

USEFUL RECEIPTS

CLEANING PICTURES

Dilute in some plain water enough gum to slightly thicken it. Soak in the liquid a pad of woollen stuff, and rub gently over stains or traces of smoke, &c. Before it dries, wash over the picture with clean water and a sponge. Dry with a smooth white cloth.

For the simple cleaning of dust from a valuable oil painting, I prefer the method which artists themselves use to clean their own work. A bowl of tepid water, with a little soft soap worked into a lather, and a sponge. Pass this over the painting gently, and wipe afterwards with a soft, clean cloth, touching lightly.

Painting on glass comes up well if you use bicarbonate of soda, which will dissolve in warm water; the solution ought to be very strong. Wash the glasses with that mixture; half an hour afterwards rub with a dry towel.

USEFUL RECEIPTS

CLEANING COPPER

*L*ight copper must be cleaned with a bit of new coal. Follow afterwards with a woollen cloth.

Old copper should be wetted with strong ammonia and then brushed well. After five minutes' work the copper is clear and bright, like new.

It is a great mistake to clean copper with acids, as to do so tarnishes them. The juice of a lemon mixed with whiting - which neutralises the acid - cleans well hangings of copper. Polish with a chamois leather. Rub with sweet oil mixed with soap. A paste of oil and pulverised pumice stone is even better. Dry with a clean towel.

USEFUL RECEIPTS

SOME GENERAL COUNSELS

*B*efore undertaking a cleaning, make sure that you have everything necessary at hand: dusters, brushes, soaps, feather brushes, old newspapers, hammer, nails - there must always be a few necessary tools in a well-managed house.

Try to choose a fine day for your cleaning. Begin, more especially in the spring cleaning, by having all the chimneys swept.

To take from the ceilings traces of smoke from the lamp or fire, wash with soft towels soaked in water in which you have dissolved a little soda.

Faded green blinds can be made to look like new by rubbing them with a rag steeped in linseed oil.

Clean chamois leather or doe-skin by washing them like cloths, but take care that the water is only lukewarm. To give them flexibility, rub them with the hands when they are dry.

THE ETIQUETTE COLLECTION
Collect the set!
ETIQUETTE FOR COFFEE LOVERS
Fresh coffee - the best welcome in the world!
Enjoy the story of coffee drinking,
coffee etiquette and recipes.

ETIQUETTE FOR CHOCOLATE LOVERS
Temptation through the years.
A special treat for all Chocolate Lovers.

THE ETIQUETTE OF NAMING THE BABY
'A good name keeps its lustre in the dark.'
Old English Proverb

THE ETIQUETTE OF AN ENGLISH TEA
How to serve a perfect English afternoon tea;
traditions, superstitions, recipes and how to read your
fortune in the tea-leaves afterwards.

THE ETIQUETTE OF ENGLISH PUDDINGS
Traditional recipes for good old-fashioned
puddings - together with etiquette notes for serving.

ETIQUETTE FOR GENTLEMEN
*'If you have occasion to use your handkerchief
do so as noiselessly as possible.'*

Copper Beech Gift Books
are designed and printed
in Great Britain